Fine Art Studio
Pastels

By Mary Iverson

Silver Dolphin Books
An imprint of the Advantage Publishers Group
5880 Oberlin Drive, San Diego, CA 92121-4794
www.silverdolphinbooks.com

Text copyright © 2007 by becker&mayer!

Fine Art Studio: Pastels is produced by becker&mayer!,
Bellevue, Washington
www.beckermayer.com

If you have questions or comments about this product, please visit www.beckermayer.com/customerservice.html and click on the Customer Service Request Form

Copyright under International, Pan American, and Universal Copyright Conventions. All rights reserved. No part of this book may be reproduced or transmitted in any form or by any means, electronic or mechanical, including photocopying, recording, or by any information storage-and-retrieval system, without written permission from the copyright holder.

ISBN-13: 978-1-59223-762-3
ISBN-10: 1-59223-762-2

Produced, manufactured, and assembled in China.

1 2 3 4 5 11 10 09 08 07

06351

Edited by Nancy Waddell
Written and illustrated by Mary Iverson
Art direction by Eddee Helms
Design assistance by Nathan Cavanaugh
Packaging design by Scott Westgard and Eddee Helms
Product development by Lauren Saint
Production management by Katie Stephens
Project management by Beth Lenz and Wendy Carmical
Photo research by Zena Chew
Special thanks to Lillis Taylor and Breanna Guidotti

Image Credits
Every effort has been made to correctly attribute all the material reproduced in this book. We will be happy to correct any errors in future editions.

Page 3: Edgar Degas, *Before the Race* © LeFevre Fine Art Ltd. / The Bridgeman Art Library / Getty Images; Frances Treanor, *Spring Symphony* © The Bridgeman Art Library / Getty Images.

Page 4: Rosalba Carriera, *Air* © Erich Lessing / Art Resource, NY; Jean Francois Millet, *The Gleaners* © Dover Publications, Inc.

Page 5: Claude Monet, *Waterloo Bridge, London* © Gérard Blot / Réunion des Musées Nationaux / Art Resource, NY; Edgar Degas, *Seated Dancer* © Giraudon / The Bridgeman Art Library / Getty Images; Breanna Guidotti, *Untitled (Giraffe).*

Page 16: Adolf Hölzel, *Composition* © Erich Lessing / Art Resource, NY.

Page 17: Leonardo da Vinci, *Mona Lisa*; Leonardo da Vinci, *Study of a Child's Head* © Lauros / The Bridgeman Art Library / Getty Images; Pierre Auguste Renoir, *After the Bath* © The Bridgeman Art Library / Getty Images; Pierre Auguste Renoir, *The Two Sisters* © The Bridgeman Art Library / Getty Images.

Page 19: Michael Dickter, *Flying Home*.

Page 20: Edgar Degas, *Two Dancers Resting* © Christie's Images / The Bridgeman Art Library / Getty Images; Edgar Degas, *Self Portrait* © Giraudon / The Bridgeman Art Library / Getty Images.

Page 21: Edgar Degas, *On the Beach at the Seashore, Three Sailboats in the Distance* © Jean Schormans / Réunion des Musées Nationaux / Art Resource, NY.

Page 23: Susan Boye, *The Olive Grove*; Tina Fong, *Ruby Mountains*.

Page 24: Roy DeForest, *Untitled (Dog)* © Weatherspoon Art Museum, University of North Carolina at Greensboro. Courtesy of George Adams Gallery, New York, and the artist; Geoffrey Robinson, *Dog 1* © The Bridgeman Art Library / Getty Images.

Page 27: Tina Fong, *Pluto*; Peilin Nee, *Mina*.

Page 28: Odilon Redon, *Vase of Flowers* © Giraudon / The Bridgeman Art Library / Getty Images; Pirjo Berg, *Flowers*.

Page 33: Michael Dickter, *Seed*; Susan Boye, *Lisbeth's Kitchen*.

Page 34: Vincent van Gogh, *Bedroom at Arles* © Dover Publications, Inc.; Michael Dickter, *The Thing About Memory*.

Page 39: Jim Stoccardo, *City Garden*; Amy Harris, *Studio 17*.

The Best of Both Worlds

If you love color and enjoy drawing, pastels are for you. With pastels, you can work on paper like you would when drawing, and at the same time mix colors the way you would when painting—it's the best of both worlds.

The rainbow array of pastel colors is irresistible, like a box of your favorite candy, tempting you to pick up a piece. Unlike paints, which are cloaked in tubes and tins, you can lift a pastel out of the box and hold the color right in your hand. There is no intermediate step of fussing with brushes, mediums, and water, as is required in painting. With pastels, you can just follow your impulse, pick up your favorite chalk, and drag it across the page to create a delicious path of color. You can make a wide range of lines and marks with pastels. If you vary how you hold the pastel, how you move your hand—twisting or turning it while you draw—and changing how hard you press, your lines take on a variety of styles. You can also blend your lines by smudging them together with your finger or by rubbing the colors with a piece of tissue.

Let this colorful collection be a bridge between your imagination and a beautiful work of art.

Edgar Degas *Before the Race*, 1893. Pastel, 24.5 x 28 in. Private collection.

Frances Treanor, *Spring Symphony*. Pastel on paper, 23 x 30 in. Private collection.

Table of Contents

History of Pastels…………………4	Color and Texture…………16
The World of Pastels……………6	Landscape………………20
What's in Your Kit?………………8	Portraiture………………24
Basic Pastel Techniques………10	Still Life…………………28
The Color Wheel………………14	My Room…………………34
	Rainbow in a Box…………40

History of Pastels

Rosalba Carriera, *Air: One of a Series of the Four Elements*, 1744. Pastel on paper, 22 x 18 in. Gemaeldegalerie, Staatliche Kunstammlungen, Dresden, Germany.

Jean-Francois Millet, *The Gleaners*, 1857. Oil on canvas, 33 x 44 in. Musée d'Orsay, Paris, France.

Portraiture

Pastels were invented in the early 1500s. At first, artists used pastels only to make preliminary sketches and studies for larger paintings. Leonardo da Vinci did this often. Some of his early studies in pastel are now hanging in museums and are considered major works of art. Over time, pastels became an acceptable medium for finished works of art, not just for sketching. In the 18th century, portraiture was the most common way to use pastels. Rosalba Carriera was a well-known portrait artist in 18th-century Europe, and sitting for a portrait by her was very fashionable. Her portrait titled *Air: One of a Series of the Four Elements* is a perfect example of how pastels can be blended to create beautiful, velvety skin tones and satiny fabrics. This soft texture can't be achieved with any other medium.

Everyday Scenes

One hundred years later, Jean-Francois Millet made his contribution to the changing ideals in art. He grew up on a small farm in France, where his family worked hard and didn't have much money. When he became an artist, he didn't agree with the popular ideas about art. At this time, artists favored dramatic scenes that celebrated the aristocracy. Millet thought that real life, the way he saw it, with people working hard in the fields, was beautiful. He used pastels in his studio to paint the scenes of poor larborers and farmers working in the field. He painted scenes he saw on a daily basis, as in *The Gleaners*.

IN THE EARLY DAYS
When pastels were first introduced, they were used only for sketches and not for "true" works of art.

Claude Monet, *Waterloo Bridge, London* circa 1900. Pastel, 12 x 19 in. Louvre, Paris, France.

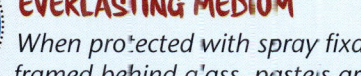

EVERLASTING MEDIUM
When protected with spray fixative or framed behind glass, pastels are the most permanent of all media. Oil paintings sometimes crack or turn yellow and watercolors can fade, but if you use high-quality paper, your pastel drawings can last forever.

Breanna Guidotti, *Untitled (Giraffe)*, 2006. Pastel on paper collage, 18 x 11.75 in.

Landscape

Inspired by Millet's outdoor scenes, the next generation of artists—the Impressionists—took pastels one step further. They carried their pastels out of doors to create spontaneous and colorful landscape paintings showing their views of the world. They loved using pastels to capture the colors of a special time of day or a season and had to work quickly to keep up with the changing light. This quick method shows up in the action-filled marks of Impressionistic drawings and is very different from the perfectly blended work of earlier portrait artists. Artists like Claude Monet carried light, portable pastel kits to sunny spots in the countryside to create sketches and on-the-spot masterpieces, such as this painting of the Waterloo Bridge—a subject that Monet came back to again and again.

Edgar Degas, *Seated Dancer*, 1881–83. Pastel on paper, 24.5 x 19 in. Musée d'Orsay, Paris, France.

The Ballet

Edgar Degas, another Impressionist, created lively, fluttering pastel paintings of the ballet. Much practice and many sketches went into the creation of one of his ballerina paintings. He attended ballet performances and practices, bringing his pastel kit with him to make quick studies. He also had dancers pose for him in his studio, where he could make more careful drawings.

Collage

Modern artists use pastels in all sorts of ways, sometimes mixing them with other art materials. Soft pastels can be used on top of a watercolor painting—once it's dry!—to heighten color or to add texture and details. Oil pastels can be added to an oil painting at any stage. Another fun thing to do with pastels is to make a collage. Artists like Pablo Picasso glued layers of paper (sometimes even newspaper) onto drawings and sketched over the layers with pastels and charcoal, much like our contemporary example seen here.

The World of Pastels

There are three kinds of pastels: soft, hard, and oil. All varieties are made by mixing powdered pigments (the same pigments that are in paint) with oil or gum arabic (a sticky liquid that's like honey). They are either rolled into round sticks or poured into molds to make square sticks.

Traditionally, artists make the first lines of a drawing using hard pastels; soft pastels are used toward the end to add gentle touches to the paper for highlights, texture, and details. When layering colors in a drawing, it's easy to add soft pastels over hard but not the other way around, because the hard pastel pigment stick will scrape off the soft.

SMUDGE-PROOFING
Accidental smearing happens often during the creation of a pastel drawing. To prevent this, you can place an extra piece of paper on top of your drawing where you rest your hand.

"There is no must in art because art is free."
—Wassily Kandinsky

Soft Pastels

Soft pastels usually come in round sticks. They have a lot of powdered pigment in them and not much gum arabic. This makes them crumbly and delicate, but also very easy to blend.

Soft pastels blend easily.

Hard pastels

Hard pastels usually come in rectangular sticks but can also be found in pencil form. Hard pastels are sturdier than soft pastels and require that you draw with a little more pressure on the paper to make a mark. They blend nicely, but not as smoothly as soft pastels.

Hard pastels create crisp lines.

Oil Pastels

The pigment in oil pastels is mixed with mineral oil instead of gum arabic. Oil pastels are like oil paint but in the form of a bright, sticky crayon. Like oil paint, you can dilute oil pastels by dipping the tips in turpentine or by blending them with a brush dipped in mineral spirits. Unlike oil paint, however, oil pastels never dry. So, if you create something special, protect it with a frame and a piece of glass.

Oil pastels cover all of the white areas.

Dry pastels show the texture of the paper.

TONE IT UP

Some artists like to use colored paper because it can harmonize with the colors of a drawing and help certain shades of pastels stand out. For example, yellow pastel looks brighter drawn on dark blue paper than on cream-colored paper.

Paper with Pizzazz

Pastels are used on special kinds of paper and sometimes on other surfaces like cardboard and sandpaper. Pastel papers have what is called a "tooth." If you looked at a piece of pastel paper under a microscope, you would see ridges, bumps, and hollows. This texture helps scrape the pigment off of the pastel stick when you draw with it across the paper. The grooves hold the pigment in place.

Pastel paper

Sandpaper

Cardboard

Tip: Pastel drawings are not as durable as a painting on canvas. To keep your drawings safe, you can make a simple portfolio out of two pieces of cardboard. Place two pieces next to each other on a table or on the floor. Line them up carefully, and tape them together lengthwise. You can fold the pieces together at the taped seam for a simple flat portfolio. Clips or pieces of tape can be used to secure the portfolio.

What's in Your Kit?

Pastels

The 22 pastels in your kit are somewhere between hard and soft pastels. This makes them both easy to draw with *and* easy to blend.

THE COLORS IN BETWEEN

Imagine what colors might exist in between the pastel colors in your kit. Blending colors together to create these intermediate colors will give you a wider range of colors to use. This will give your artwork a more cohesive feel.

Tip: Use a regular pencil sharpener to shave the wood down and expose the charcoal tip. Then, with a sanding block or an emery board, file the tip of your charcoal pencil down to a fine point.

use your charcoal pencil to sketch out basic shapes.

Charcoal Pencil

Charcoal looks a lot like pastel, but it is made from burned wood instead of powdered pigments. Many artists use charcoal at the beginning of a drawing to sketch out basic shapes. Your charcoal pencil can be sharpened, which will be useful when adding details or sketching fine lines in your drawings.

Blending Stump

Your blending stump is a rolled piece of paper with a point at each end that can be sharpened with sandpaper. Rub it into pastels and charcoal to create smoothly blended areas. You can also draw with your blending stump to create soft, fuzzy lines.

Your blending stump has a variety of uses.

TIP: For a softer touch, you can use a soft paintbrush or a secondhand makeup brush to blend your colors.

Blending Brush

Pastel artists love the soft blended effects created with a blending brush! This brush is a lot like a paintbrush, but the hairs are cut off bluntly at the end. Use it to soften hard edges or to brush loose pigment off of your drawing.

Viewfinder

The viewfinder in your kit is a tool you will use to learn about perspective and composition. Artists use perspective to add depth to their drawings and to make objects look three-dimensional.

Paper

Pastel paper, available at art supply stores, comes in a variety of colors from light to bright. Your kit has five sheets, one for each project.

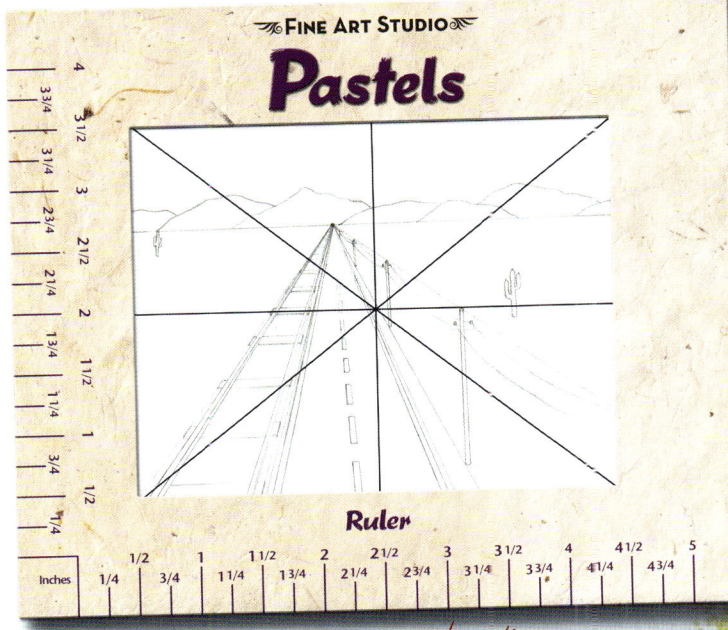

Diagonal perspective lines create space in a drawing.

9

Basic Pastel Techniques

The first impulse in drawing with pastels is to make lines. There are many kinds of lines and marks you can make with your pastel sticks.

You can use the tip of the pastel stick to draw a simple line or use the side to create wide bands of color. Your marks can be slow and smooth or quick and fluttering. The kinds of marks you make in a drawing will affect the piece as a whole. If you use only quick, short marks, your drawing might communicate the feeling of excitement. If you use only long, swooping lines, your drawing may have a languid feel to it, inspiring someone to smile or relax. How would your drawing look if you used only sidestrokes?

"I try to apply colors like words that shape poems, like notes that shape music."
—Joan Miro

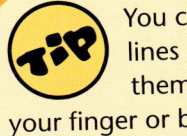

Tip: You can blend your lines by smudging them together with your finger or by rubbing the colors together with a piece of tissue.

Bold
Hold your hand steady to create a bold line.

Flickering
Flick your wrist to make energetic marks.

Static
Tap the tip of your pastel on the paper for these spotty marks.

Twisted
Turn your hand midstroke to make this twisty line.

Wavy
Let your hand be loose and light for this curvy line.

Crosshatching

This is a technique used to build up areas of color using only lines.

1 To crosshatch, draw a set of short parallel lines in one direction, then add a second set over the top but in a different direction, either perpendicular or at an angle to the original set.

2 You can fill an area with many of these crosshatched patches and even lay patches of different colors over one another.

3 After several layers, you end up with a patch of textured color.

Erasing

Using an eraser is a fun way to make marks. Experiment with this technique by starting with a toned ground (see page 13), then pulling an eraser through it to make lines and squiggles. What would happen if you started with a piece of colored paper?

Tip: To get the best textured effects, use your pastel stick directly on the textured surface. Blending techniques, such as rubbing the pigment with your finger or using a blending stump, won't create much texture.

Texturizing

The powdery character of pastels makes them very responsive to the drawing surface. You can achieve a variety of textured effects by experimenting with different types of paper, or even cardboard.

Drawing on textured paper will leave little white spots of paper showing through the color.

Smooth paper will give your drawing an overall even tone.

If you draw on cardboard, you will see stripes!

Blending

Use blending techniques when you need to create a smooth, continuous area of color in your drawing or when you want to soften some edges. This is helpful when you want to draw the sky, a large area of color like a wall or tabletop, or soft, smooth elements, like fabric.

Begin by making a cluster of lines of any kind, then use your fingers, blending brush, or blending stump to spread out the marks and make a smooth color.

You can use your finger to blend lines.

This technique is useful when you want two colors to fade into each other.

Building Up

Pastel artists usually develop their drawings using many layers of color. This is called *building up*. If you start with a toned ground, you can add colors on top of it to build up the layers. Begin by blocking in the large shapes, and work toward the details, like highlights and textured lines.

FIXING

Because pastels are so powdery and don't stick to the paper like paint does, it's important to take good care of your favorite drawings. One way of doing this is to use a fixative spray (available at art supply stores). This spray acts like glue and adheres the powdery pigment to the paper. Use light, thin coats of fixative; heavy spraying might change the colors in your drawing. Some artists like to fix their drawings in the early stages of working on them, to keep underlying areas from smearing. Be sure to ask an adult for help when you are using fixative.

Toned Ground

Sometimes it's nice to start with color on the paper to help set a mood for your drawing. Use blending techniques to spread a light layer of one color across the entire piece of paper. You can also create a toned ground with two colors.

1 Start with Two Colors

2 Blend the Colors

3 Add Details

Colored Paper

Another way of beginning with a toned ground is to use colored paper.

You can also use dark pastels on light-colored paper.

Start with a dark-colored piece of paper and add light-colored marks.

13

The Color Wheel

If you take all of the colors of the rainbow and wrap them into a circle, you have a *color wheel*. When choosing colors for a painting or drawing, it is helpful to look at where they are on this circle.

Tip: You can plan the color scheme for your drawing ahead of time, or you can just go by feel. Sometimes it's fun to see what kinds of color schemes you choose naturally.

Can you arrange the pastels in your kit into a color wheel?

Complementary Colors

A complementary color scheme uses two colors that are opposite each other on the color wheel.

Triadic Colors

If you draw a triangle in the color wheel, the three colors at its tips can make a triadic color scheme.

Color Schemes

Color scheme is the term used to describe the handful of colors used in a work of art. There are some popular color schemes that can be mapped out on the color wheel: monochromatic, analogous, triadic, and complementary.

Analogous
The analogous color scheme uses colors that are right next to each other on the color wheel, like the yellow and green seen here.

Monochromatic
Paintings that use a single color and its hues are called *monochromatic*, which means "one color."

Complementary
Orange and blue are the two complementary colors in this color scheme.

Triadic
This triadiac color palette features orange, purple, and green.

COLORS AND FEELINGS
Colors have meaning beyond what we see with our eyes, and many artists use colors to add an emotional charge or deeper meaning to their drawings and paintings.

15

Color and Texture

Adolf Hölzel was a German artist born in 1853. Hölzel created art to convey his inner world. His style is called *nonrepresentational*, meaning that he didn't draw pictures of actual objects or of anything recognizable.

Early in his career, he worked in an Impressionistic style. As he continued working, he focused more and more on the idea that colors and shapes describe feelings better than any picture of real-world objects or people. This approach to making art is called Expressionism. Hölzel's drawings are color studies with spirals and circles that overlap, full of colorful patches inside intersecting lines. In addition to painting and drawing, Hölzel created designs for stained-glass windows.

Adolf Hölzel, Color Expert

Adolf Hölzel, *Composition*, 1927–28. Chalk on paper, 21 x 27 in. Museum am Ostwall, Dortmund, Germany.

This drawing, *Composition*, looks like a stained-glass window. Imagine that you could look through a window and see your innermost thoughts and feelings. What would you see?

You might find a cluster of beautiful colors, a collection of memories, or an array of feelings. Stories could be unfolding behind the panes of glass, like in a dream.

"The aim of art is to represent not the outward appearance of things, but their inward significance."
—Aristotle

Sketchy Evidence

It is fun to see evidence of the early stages of planning for a painting. Seeing the sketchy lines and rough diagrams that Leonardo da Vinci jotted down in his pastel studies is like getting a glimpse into his imagination. It reminds us that works like the *Mona Lisa* required careful preparatory studies.

But pastels are not used just for sketching anymore. Since they are similar to a pencil, it makes sense to use them to sketch and draw. Because you are able to mix colors, it can seem a lot like painting. It is this combination of qualities that makes working with pastels a unique experience in the world of art. It's the best of both worlds: drawing and painting.

Leonardo da Vinci, *Mona Lisa*, 1503–06. Oil on panel, 30 x 21 in. Louvre, Paris, France.

Leonardo da Vinci, *Study of a Child's Head*. Chalk on paper. Musée des Beaux-Arts, Caen, France.

Is It Drawing or Painting?

Because pastels can be used in both ways, some works of art made with pastels are called pastel drawings, while others are called pastel paintings. What is the difference? When the work is sketchy and areas of paper are showing, it's called a pastel drawing. When every inch of the paper is covered with blended pastel, it can be called a pastel painting.

Pierre Auguste Renoir, *After the Bath*, 1890. Pastel on paper, 26 x 21 in. Leeds Museums and Galleries, U.K.

See how Renoir left the outer edges of the paper uncovered by pastel. The beige color of the paper adds another layer of color that enhances this pastel drawing.

In this portrait, Renoir chose to cover the entire piece of paper with pastel. It is considered a pastel painting.

Pierre Auguste Renoir, *The Two Sisters*. Pastel on paper, 31 x 25 in. Briston City Museum and Art Gallery, U.K.

Colors I Love

Do you have a favorite color? How does it make you feel when you see it? In this exercise, you will focus on color and the different feelings it evokes in you.

Materials
- PASTELS
- PAPER
- BLENDING BRUSH
- BLENDING STUMP
- TISSUE FOR BLENDING

1 Pick Your Colors

Take a look at the set of pastels in your kit and pick seven that you like. Pick them quickly by how they make you feel—don't think too much as you make your choices.

Organize these colors into dark colors and light colors. For example, purple and brown are dark colors; yellow and light blue are light colors.

COLOR CHOICE
Do you know that 75 percent of kids say purple is their favorite color? Are you surprised by what colors you picked? Do you think they go together?

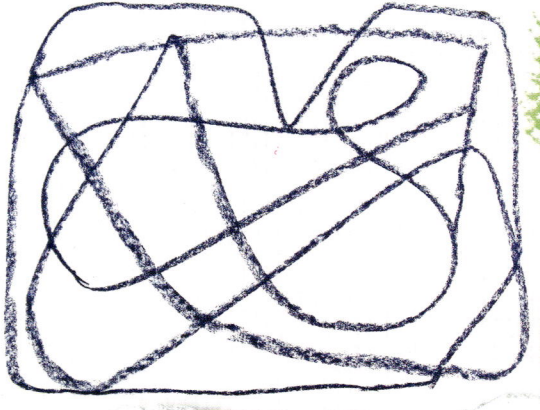

2 Create a Design

Choose one of your darker colors. In our example, we started with purple. Begin your drawing by creating a design of swirling lines filling the page. Leave some shapes open.

3 Fill in the Spaces

Use crosshatching and blending techniques to add colors to the spaces between your swirly lines.

Work until you have covered your entire page with color.

Tip
In our example, there is a lot of light green in the center, with dark shapes wrapping around the outside: The greens, yellows, and purples might suggest springtime flowers and warm sunshine.

4 Stand Back

Pin your drawing to a wall and stand back. How does it make you feel? Are there any patterns of movement or color that you can see?

5 Add a Layer

Add another layer of color to the areas you noticed while standing back from your drawing. This will enhance the idea of movement in your drawing.

TIP: We added green marks to give texture to one of the light green shapes and to make it unique from the other shapes like it. Some of the outlines were made lighter and some darker to accent those lines. You can use new colors from your kit as accents.

Well Done!

TIP: We added color to the outside edges, blending from sunny orange to green to give the feeling of sunshine on spring leaves.

"I never get tired of the blue sky."
—Vincent van Gogh

Michael Dickter

This simple composition of gold, blue, and black asks the viewer to decipher its meaning. There seems to be a story being told by the two seeds glued to the page. One seed looks like a bird flying in a sun-drenched sky, and the other is a figure at rest on the black shape. The blue band of color looks like it could be a distant hillside. Is this the "home" to where the seed is flying?

Michael Dickter, *Flying Home*. Pastel and mixed media on paper.

Landscape

Edgar Degas was born in Paris in 1834. He worked in an Impressionistic style and exhibited his paintings with other Impressionists in Paris. In contrast to this group of artists who enjoyed working outdoors, Degas liked to work in his studio. He made pastel sketches of his subjects on the spot but created paintings later in the comfort of his studio.

Degas chose to use pastels, as they worked well for his delicate and careful studies and also because he could work quickly with them when he was on location. He took advantage of the way pastel paintings can be developed in layers, and worked with the medium in a way similar to how the other Impressionists used their paints.

Edgar Degas, *Two Dancers Resting*, 1874. Pastel. Private collection.

Edgar Degas, *Self Portrait*, 1862. Oil on canvas, 36 x 27 in. Museu Calouste Gulbenkian, Lisbon, Portugal.

Edgar Degas, Draftsman

Like Alfred Hölzel, Edgar Degas used line, color, and shape to evoke feeling. Degas, however, set up his patterns of interlocking lines by means of posing the human figure. In *Two Dancers Resting*, the arms and legs of the dancers set up a stream of motion that makes your eyes dart around the painting. The colored shapes are still there, but in Degas's work they have looser edges and blend into one another.

"Painting is easy when you don't know how, but very difficult when you do."
—Edgar Degas

Easy Landscape

This exercise will increase your skill at blending and give you the opportunity to make a toned ground. You'll also be able to use your imagination to set up a realistic scene.

Materials

- PAPER
- PASTELS
- TISSUE FOR BLENDING
- BLENDING STUMP
- BLENDING BRUSH
- CHARCOAL PENCIL

Edgar Degas, By the Sea

Edgar Degas, *On the Beach at the Seashore, Three Sailboats in the Distance*, 1869. Pastel on paper. Louvre, Paris, France.

In this seascape by Degas, there are three main areas of color: the sky, the water, and the sandy beach. Underneath these areas is a brown toned ground. You can see spots of it peeking through the sky and the beach.

1 Create a Toned Ground

Using your brown pastel, spread a light amount of pigment across your paper.

Rub it in and smooth it around the paper with a tissue—or your fingers—to get an even expanse of brown.

2 Block in Color

For the sky, start with lots of strokes using your turquoise pastel stick.

Over this color, apply crosshatching lines of light blue and a little bit of yellow. You might want to try this on a piece of scrap paper first to get just the right combination.

Blend the patches together with your blending stump—or your fingers—to get a smooth blue sky.

Tip: The sky doesn't always have to be blue. You can try unusual colors for the sky, like yellow or green, to give your drawing extra pizzazz.

For the water, use the same technique that you used for the sky, but use more white in the area where the water and the sky are touching.

For the beach, use yellow ocher, light yellow, and a little bit of brown. Blend them together.

3 Add Clouds

With your white pastel, add some patches of white to the sky. Make these clouds larger and whiter toward the top of the page.

Closer to the water, use less white and make smaller shapes for distant clouds that blend more into the sky.

Use your blending brush to soften the edges. This will help make the clouds look fluffy.

4 Add Waves

Add dark and light wave shapes to the sea using the same method you used to make the clouds in step 3.

TIP: Remember that objects in the distance appear smaller. Your waves and clouds should decrease in size and be closer together as they get farther away.

5 Create a Beach

To create the texture of a sandy beach, you can use the rubbing technique.

Place your paper over an object that has texture—like a flat, rough rock or a piece of wood—and draw on top of it. Does the texture of the object come through?

TIP: You can also use your charcoal pencil to make simple marks in the foreground to suggest things such as rocks and driftwood.

Add the Boats!

TIP
Degas used very simple shapes to make the boats in his drawing. On a separate piece of paper, practice drawing small boats. Use just a few lines and marks for each boat. Use your blending brush to soften the edges of the boats.

MORE EASY LANDSCAPE IDEAS
You can use the techniques in this exercise to draw views of different places. For example, you can create a simple landscape with broad fields, a blue sky, and a little barn in the distance. Can you think of any other simple scenes?

Susan Boye
In this landscape, Boye played with the textural qualities of pastels. She created soft outlines around all of the shapes by building up layers of colorful marks. Looking at this painting, the viewer gets the feeling that autumn has wrapped the scene in a warm, fuzzy blanket.

Susan Boye, *The Olive Grove*, 1997. Pastel on paper, 22 x 30 in.

Tina Fong, *Ruby Mountains*, 2002. Pastel on paper, 10.5 x 9 in.

Tina Fong
This dramatic landscape was inspired by the Ruby Mountains in Nevada. Fong, who is fond of open landscapes and desert areas, started with a photograph she had taken on a trip to the desert. In her pastel painting, Fong embellished upon the already moody scene. Her dark, ominous clouds suggest strong emotions. What colors do you think this artist loves?

Portraiture

The theme of a work of art or the items featured within a painting or drawing is sometimes called *subject matter*. Many artists are very fond of one particular subject and make studies of it over and over again. For Monet, water lilies were a continual source of inspiration. Degas focused on ballet dancers. Van Gogh painted his own portrait many times. If there is anything you are fascinated with or that you love to look at, it would make a great subject for a pastel drawing or painting.

Roy DeForest is an artist who paints a really lovable subject: his dogs! He was born in 1930 in Nebraska and grew up in Washington State. His early work was a lot like that of Alfred Hölzel, with overlapping shapes and colors, but it evolved to become more representational. He held onto the bright colors and fun patterns but added images from his life, including his animals.

Roy DeForest, *Untitled (Dog)*, 1975. Pastel, watercolor, charcoal, and colored pencil on paper, 22.5 x 30.125 in. Weatherspoon Art Museum, Greensboro, North Carolina.

Roy DeForest, Animal Lover

Roy DeForest creates paintings and drawings of his dogs in a brightly colored, playful style. In his drawings, he often takes his grinning canines on playful journeys through magical, dreamlike places. He works from his imagination and from reality, using colors he loves and shapes and symbols from his dreams along with realistic sketches of his animals.

Where do you think the dog in Roy DeForest's drawing is? It looks like he's in some kind of landscape with a palm tree and some clouds. What do you think the pictures of other dogs at the top mean? Maybe the dog is thinking about his friends.

Geoffrey Robinson, *Dog 1*, 1994. Pastel on paper. Private collection.

"For me, one of the most beautiful things about art is that it is one of the last strongholds of magic."
—Roy DeForest

Pet Portrait

In this exercise, you will use line and color to explore the subject of animals. Because it is tough to get your pet to sit still (unless he or she is an excellent sleeper), you might want to use a photograph. If you don't have a pet, you can use a picture of an animal from a magazine, or a photograph of a friend's pet.

Materials

- PHOTOGRAPH OF YOUR PET OR AN ANIMAL YOU LIKE
- CHARCOAL PENCIL
- SCRAP PAPER
- VIEWFINDER
- PAPER
- PASTELS

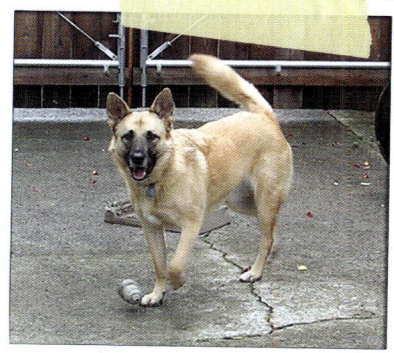

Make some small sketches of your pet using different compositions.

1 Practice Sketching

On a piece of scrap paper, experiment with different ways of drawing your animal.

Use your charcoal pencil to make some practice sketches. Focus on the eyes, nose, and ears.

Do you want to include the whole body or just the head and shoulders?

2 Experiment

Composition refers to where the subject of a painting or drawing sits on the page. You can center your portrait on the page or have it coming in from the side. Your portrait can be large and in the front, or small toward the top of the page. How about moving it to the left or right?

A close-up view might convey intimacy and love.

A more distant view would be better for showing action.

USING YOUR VIEWFINDER

Hold your viewfinder in front of your eyes and look through it toward your subject. If you move the viewfinder closer to your face, the subject becomes smaller within the rectangle. When you move the viewfinder away from your face, the subject fills up the frame. Which view do you like better? Does one view communicate a different message than the other?

3 Choose a Composition

Once you've had some practice sketching your animal, you can begin to work on your pastel drawing.

Pick your favorite composition sketch and use your charcoal pencil to copy that drawing onto your paper.

TIP It helps to keep a notebook with you, so you can practice sketching whenever you feel inspired. You can sketch things you see, or things you imagine. Either way, it's great practice and will keep your creative ideas flowing.

4 Add Feeling

At this point, your drawing has a lot of blank space in it. You'll need to come up with some elements to fill that space.

Think about your animal and how you feel about it. While keeping that in mind, play with your colors and see what shapes you are inspired to make. These can be colorful shapes and symbols like stars, swirls, or patches of color; or they can be images that tell a story about where your animal is and what it is doing.

5 Add Details

What kinds of things do you and your pet like to do? Have you been on any adventures together? Do you imagine your pet traveling anywhere?

Pull It All Together!

TIP Take a look at the drawing as a whole to see if there are any blank spaces that need filling or any elements that need to be pulled together. Make sure your portrait illustrates how you feel about your subject.

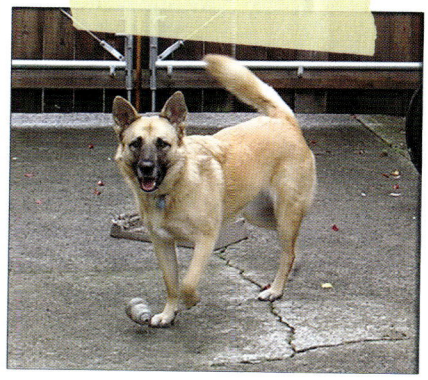

Tina Fong
To begin this realistic pet portrait, Fong sketched the form of the dog on beige-colored paper. Next, she added the dark areas and worked her way to the lights. The smoky darks give this dog's eyes a mysterious look.

Tina Fong, *Pluto*, 2001. Pastel on paper, 10.5 x 9 in.

Peilin Nee
In this close-up portrait, the artist gives us a deep look into the cat's green eyes. If Nee were using a viewfinder to come up with this composition, she would have had to hold it right next to the cat's face. Blue, yellow-green, and orange give this painting a triadic color scheme.

Peilin Nee, *Mina*, 2005. Pastel on paper, 6.5 x 4.5 in.

27

Still Life

Odilon Redon was an artist well known for his imaginative, dreamlike creations. He was born in France in 1840 and liked to draw mystical creatures and strange, imaginative things you might encounter in dreams. This style of working with dreamlike imagery is called *symbolism*.

Early in his career, he worked mostly in black and white, but when he was 50 years old he switched to using pastels for his drawings. His work with pastels brought color and new feelings into his work. Pastels made his images look even dreamier, due to the textures and smoothly blended areas he created with the powdery medium. His work also took on a misty quality. In his drawings, patches of soft color surround his subjects like a fog, giving a mysterious feeling to his work.

Odilon Redon, *Vase of Flowers*, 1912. Pastel on paper. Private collection.

Odilon Redon, Dreamer

By creating a colorful backdrop for the vase of flowers, Redon solved the problem of having lots of white paper showing around the still life while also putting a set of colors he loved into play. How do the colors of the toned ground in *Vase of Flowers* make you feel? What effect would a different set of colors have on the feeling of the piece?

Pirjo Berg, *Flowers*, 2006. Oil pastel on paper, 8 × 8 in.

"I perhaps owe having become a painter to flowers."
—Claude Monet

Colorful Still Life

In this exercise, you will use a toned ground as a background for a simple still life drawing. Many artists use a toned ground to set the mood for a drawing.

Materials
- **STILL LIFE SUBJECTS**
- **PASTELS**
- **PAPER**
- **TISSUE FOR BLENDING**
- **BLENDING BRUSH**

1 Set the Scene

Gather together some items for a simple still life setup. You will need a vase and some things to put in it, such as flowers, stalks of berries, thin branches, grasses, or leaves.

You can use real things found outdoors, or a flower arrangement from the store. Dried or silk flowers will also work. You could even try to create flowers in your mind's eye. And, there's no reason why you can't use a combination of real and imagined flowers.

TIP: If you are going to invent your flowers, it's a good idea to look at a real one to get an idea of how it is put together. There might be some interesting details you see in a real flower that you wouldn't have thought to add otherwise.

2 Pick Your Colors

Think back to the set of colors you picked in the "Colors I Love" exercise on page 18. What were they? From these, choose a dark color and a light color to use as the main colors for your toned ground. You can use the whole range of colors you love as a starting point for the color scheme in this exercise.

3 Create a Toned Ground

You will create a tabletop area below a sky-type area, using the two colors chosen in step 2. In our example, we use light blue and medium green.

First spread some of the darker color onto the bottom of the page, then spread some of the lighter color onto the top of the page.

With a tissue, a brush, or your fingers, blend these areas so that pigment covers the entire page.

Blend the colors together where they meet.

TIP When the paper is colored, you can add some variation to the ground to make things shimmer. In our drawing, we added some light yellow to the "sky" to lighten it in some areas, and some medium blue to darken it in others.

4 Draw the Vase

Outline the basic shape of the vase and fill it in with a simple color.

In our exercise, the vase is orange, with light yellow highlights and reddish-purple shadows. A mixture of purple and dark orange will match this very well.

5 Arrange the Flowers

Lightly sketch circles and ovals where you want the flowers to be.

Sketch out the entire bouquet before you begin the details of any one piece.

BOUQUET OF CIRCLES

An ellipse is the shape a circle takes on when you look at it from an angle. You can see this easily when you look at the rim of a cup. Looking straight down from above the cup, you see a circle. From the side, the top of the cup has an elliptical shape. A bouquet of flowers is full of circles and ellipses.

6 Add Details

Look at the differences among all of your flowers. Some have simple, separate petals, while others are more complicated.

Think about their underlying shapes. Some are flat, as if they are on a Frisbee, while others are round, like a ball. Add to your sketches of circles and ovals to show these differences.

Add some stems between your round shapes.

Tip: Some artists hold their drawings up in front of a mirror to get a new perspective.

7 Add More Color

Choose a range of hues for the flowers. Fill your flower leaf shapes with these colors.

Tip: You might want to try using a color scheme you read about earlier in this book. In our still life setup, we used a triadic color scheme of yellow, pink, and orange.

8 Add Shadows

In our photograph of the bouquet, you can see light and shadow.

The shadow areas are: (1) the dark area on the table next to the vase and (2) the dark areas in and around all of the flowers.

Use a dark green pastel for these areas in your drawing.

ATTENTION GRABBER

When you place your lightest and darkest areas next to each other in a drawing, you create an area of high contrast, which gets peoples' attention. Dark colors seem darker when placed next to lights, and light colors seem even lighter when next to dark colors. So if there is a bright spot in your drawing that you want people to notice, place a dark piece of color right next to it and you'll get their attention!

9 Create Highlights

Now look for the light areas on the vase, the table, and in every flower.

The glass vase is very shiny and reflects the lights in the room. Look for the very lightest white areas, or *highlights*, on the vase. Draw the highlights with your white pastel. Use your cream and light pink pastels to add some light areas. Blend with your finger.

Finished!

Tip: To make a still life that tells a story, gather together objects that relate to one theme. What kinds of objects might suggest a summer vacation? How about a favorite sport or something you like to do? For example, if you love baseball, you could arrange a bat, ball, mitt, and cap into a still life.

Susan Boye

This painting places the still life in a different setting—on a windowsill! This arrangement of a vase next to the window gives the artist an opportunity to include the view outside of the window. The terra-cotta colors and the stucco buildings suggest that the scene is set in a foreign country. What other clues does the artist give us about where and when she created this piece?

Susan Boye, *Lisbeth's Kitchen*, 1997. Pastel on paper, 22 x 30 in.

Michael Dickter, *Seed*, 2006. Pastel and charcoal on paper, 22 x 30 in.

Michael Dickter

Like a scientist, this artist observes a plant found in nature, looking at its details and recording them in a realistic pastel sketch. The earth tones give the piece a historical feeling, as if the artist had discovered a new type of plant and noted its description in a notebook.

My Room

Vincent van Gogh was born in Holland in 1853. When he was 27 years old, he abandoned his work as a preacher and missionary, and set off to paint the world his way. His painting career followed just after the time of the Impressionists, so his style was called "Postimpressionistic." The Impressionists, like Claude Monet, had broken some "rules" about painting by leaving their brushstrokes and colors unblended (so that viewers at the time considered the paintings unfinished), but van Gogh took these innovations even further, using intense colors and textures.

Van Gogh was a daring and innovative artist. His style looks normal to us today, but to his contemporaries it was radical. No one had painted quite like him before. After van Gogh's time, the rules of the art world were expanded and it became acceptable for an artist to be eccentric, to value originality above all else, and to live the adventurous lifestyle we've come to associate with artists.

Vincent van Gogh, *Bedroom at Arles*, 1889. Oil on canvas, 22.5 x 29 in. Musée d'Orsay, Paris, France.

Vincent van Gogh, Visionary

Vincent van Gogh is well known for his intensely colored paintings full of energetic brushstrokes. He almost always used oil paints, yet his paintings are so full of directional lines, they look as if they were made with pastels.

His bright, saturated colors infused what he saw through his eyes with the energy and intensity that was in his mind and in his heart. There are many stories about his inner intensity, including a story about how he cut off part of his ear!

MORE ABOUT COLOR

Saturation is the intensity of a color. When a color is pure, with no other colors or white mixed with it, it is at its maximum saturation and is very vivid. Some of the pastels in your kit are saturated colors. To lower the saturation of a color, you can mix it with some white, gray, black, or a color that sits across from it on the color wheel.

Michael Dickter, *The Thing About Memory*, 2005. Pastel and charcoal on paper, 60 x 20 in.

Perspective

Vincent van Gogh built a perspective device with strings and nails to help him draw complicated scenes. He saw that when one drew objects with parallel sides, like railroad tracks and floorboards, the angles could be connected at one point.

Tip: The angle of the side of the bed, the bottom edges of the paintings, and the line where the floor meets the ceiling all point to one vanishing point.

Vanishing Point

The viewfinder in your kit uses the same idea. If you hold it up to a scene that has lots of angles, you will find that they all meet at one central point, called the *vanishing point*. If you place your viewfinder over van Gogh's *Bedroom at Arles*, you'll find that most of the angles point toward one vanishing point.

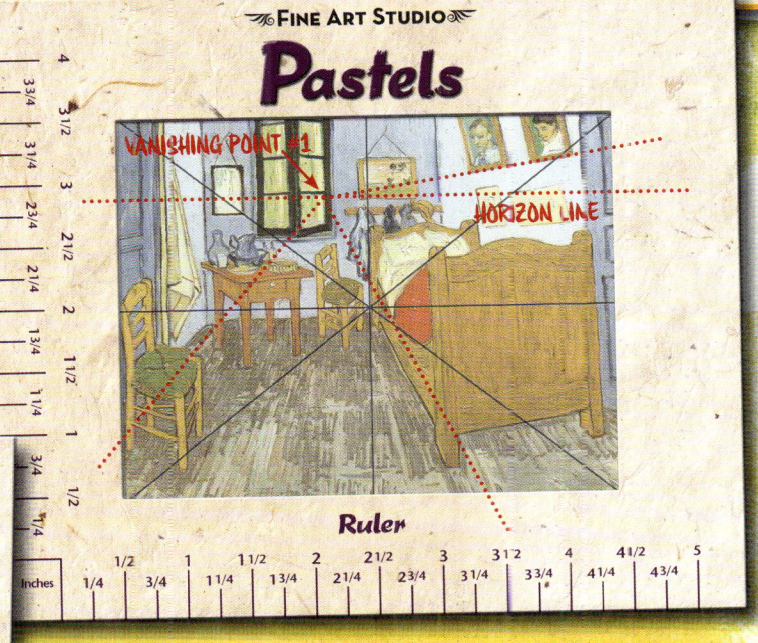

Horizon Line

Some of the angles in van Gogh's painting point in a different direction, toward a second vanishing point. If you locate these new points, you'll find that they all line up across a horizontal line. This line is called the *horizon line*.

Eye Level

The horizon line is at the same level as your eye level. The horizon line in the painting looks like it is at the level of the top of the bed's headboard. This means that van Gogh must have been sitting down when he made this painting.

My Room

In this exercise, you will learn to draw in perspective using your viewfinder. You will also use many of the concepts and techniques already discussed in this book, such as color schemes, blending, creating light and shadow, adding details, and layering colors.

Materials

- CHARCOAL PENCIL
- SCRAP PAPER
- PAPER
- VIEWFINDER
- PASTELS
- TISSUE FOR BLENDING
- BLENDING STUMP

1 Make Some Sketches

Find a spot in your room where you have a view of the whole room and, if possible, a view out a window.

Make some preliminary sketches in charcoal like you did with the pet portrait.

Use your viewfinder to look at your room from a few different spots. Sketch them out.

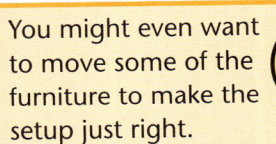

TIP

You might even want to move some of the furniture to make the setup just right.

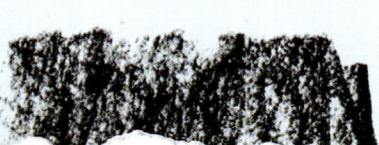

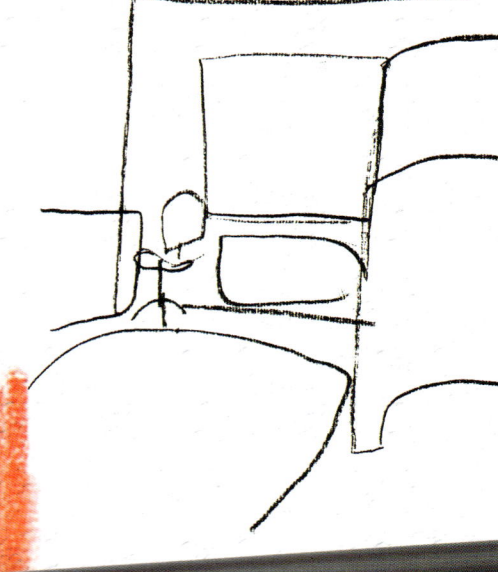

2 Choose a Sketch

Which sketch do you like best? In our example, the vertical sketch seems the most interesting because it includes the desk and both levels of the bunk bed.

Choose your favorite sketch of your room and loosely draw it out on a sheet of pastel paper. At this stage, the drawing does not need to be perfect—just focus on getting things like the furniture and the window close to the right spot.

3 Use the Viewfinder

Hold your viewfinder up to view the room. Choose one of the obvious diagonals. In our example, the edge of the rug has a long diagonal.

Without moving the pencil or your thumbs, hold this viewfinder/pencil combination up to your drawing. Do the angles match?

Go back and forth with this measurement technique, erasing and redrawing lines on your paper until you get all of the angles in the room just right.

Hold your charcoal pencil on top of your viewfinder with your thumbs, and line it up with the angle you've chosen.

Try to hold the viewfinder straight up and down, not tilted forward or backward, because this affects the angle.

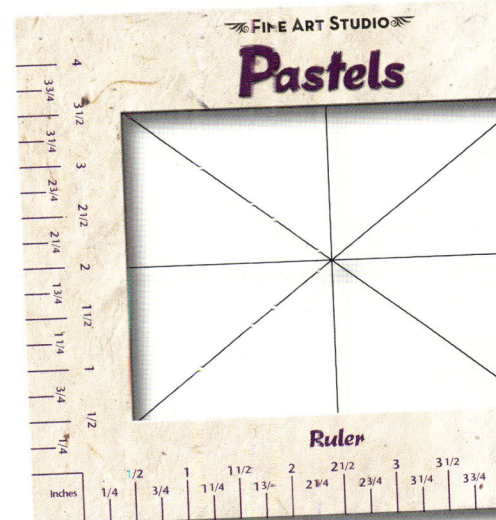

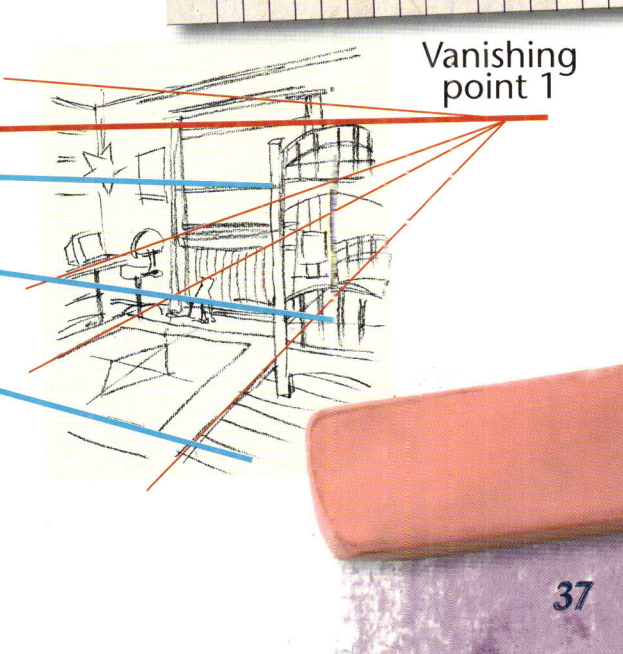

Vanishing point 2   Horizon line   Vanishing point 1

When you get all of the angles drawn, you can take a look at the perspective lines. In our example, there are two vanishing points, and both are off to the side of the drawing. The long sides of the rug and the bunk bed go to a vanishing point on the right. The other sides of the rug go to a vanishing point on the left. Notice that they are both on the same horizon line, which is at the eye level of a person who is standing up.

37

4 Begin with Color

Loosely fill in the shapes of your drawing with the colors you've chosen. Start with the large shapes first, so you can see your progress better.

ROOM WITH A VIEW

Like van Gogh's painting, we want to make our painting burst with color. Where you see blue, even if it's a grayish blue like the bunk bed, choose a blue that will stand out in your drawing. Where you see a rusty red, like in the carpet, choose a bright red from your pastel box. For browns, work with oranges and yellows. You can even change the color of something completely, if there is one you would like better.

5 Add Shadows

Look for the darkest areas in your room and add those to your painting using your charcoal pencil and dark pastels like black, dark blue, dark brown, and gray.

In our example, there is a dark shadow under the bed, under the desk, the computer screen, the cat, the side of the lamp, the radiator, the window edges, and the sides of the mattress. Some of the white areas around the window and in the curtains are touched with gray.

6 Fill in Your Shapes

Use blending techniques and extra pastel marks to fill in your shapes more tightly. You can use your finger or a tissue to spread color around the larger shapes.

To heighten the look of light and shadow in your painting, add some new, lighter colors into existing color areas. In our example, we added pink and yellow, respectively, to the red and orange of the rug.

Tip: The blending stump is great for pushing pigment into tight little corners, like between the slats of the bunk bed.

One Last Thing!

CROSSHATCHING

Crosshatching with pastels produces a unique effect; you can add a shimmery, energetic feeling to your painting. Choose colors that are similar to the ones you already used—just darker or lighter versions of them. After you've made a layer of marks with the new color, go back over them with a layer of marks using the original color. Leave your marks unblended.

TIP: The original wall color is light blue. We used the crosshatching technique and went over it with a layer of gray marks, then went back in with blue marks again.

Amy Harris, *Studio 17*, 2007. Pastel, 18 x 24 in.

Jim Stoccardo

This artist is standing on the outside, looking in. The painting includes imagined views of high-rise apartments on a busy city street. The inhabitants of the rooms can be seen going about their lives. The artist painted the sky, buildings, and street with solid areas of acrylic paint, then drew over the top with pastel pencils, adding the details of the interiors and the grass in the foreground.

Jim Stoccardo, *City Garden*, 2003. Pastel, acrylic, and charcoal on panel, 48 x 48 in.

Amy Harris

This painting is a playful view of an artist's studio. The artist combined several viewpoints into one picture to create a whimsical, wide-angle view. She added special details, like her beloved dog in its cozy bed, art projects laid out on her drawing table, paintings on the walls, and a colorful sunset outside the window.

Rainbow in a Box

When you open a box of pastels, you find an irresistible rainbow array of drawing materials that inspires creativity. Now that you have learned the basics of working with pastels, you can carry this inspiration with you in whatever you do. Whether you use pastels all of the time or along with other mediums, you can bring the inspiration of pure color to your work.

PRACTICE INSPIRATION
Keep your set of pastel sticks handy at your desk so you can sketch and practice whenever you have an idea or feel inspired. Or, take your pastels and a sketchbook with you on trips to make drawings of your adventures. Now that you've begun, the important thing is to continue to practice, keep your approach light, and have fun!